Cello Time Sprinters

a third book of pieces for cello

Kathy and David Blackwell

Grateful thanks are due to Alison Ingram and Tom Morter
for all their help with this volume.

Welcome to **Cello Time Sprinters**. You'll find:

- extended pieces in first position
- fourth position pieces using the finger patterns 1–34, 12–4, and 1234
- a range of techniques, e.g. hooked bowing, string crossing, and double-stops
- original pieces in different styles plus pieces by a range of composers
- duets with parts of equal difficulty
- scales and arpeggios to suit the pieces and at the level of Grade 3
- Performances and backings for all the pieces, many with drumkit and bass added, as well as tuning tracks, available to download from a Companion Website: www.oup.com/ctsprinters
- straightforward piano accompaniments available in a separate volume

Pieces with piano accompaniment are presented in two formats on the Companion Website: firstly, a complete performance, then the accompaniment only, which you can play along to. There is a count-in when the cello and piano parts start together.

 This symbol is placed alongside all the pieces for which audio tracks are available to download from the Companion Website. For all duets, there is a track with the top part only and a track with the lower part only, so that you can play along with either part.

 This symbol indicates which pieces have a piano accompaniment (published in a separate volume).

MUSIC DEPARTMENT

OXFORD
UNIVERSITY PRESS

T0056063

OXFORD
UNIVERSITY PRESS

Great Clarendon Street, Oxford OX2 6DP, England
198 Madison Avenue, New York, NY10016, USA

Oxford University Press is a department of the University of Oxford.
It furthers the University's aim of excellence in research, scholarship,
and education by publishing worldwide

Oxford is a registered trade mark of Oxford University Press
in the UK and in certain other countries

20

ISBN 0–19–322115–2

Music and text origination by
Barnes Music Engraving Ltd., East Sussex

Printed in Great Britain on acid-free paper by
Halstan & Co. Ltd., Amersham, Bucks.

All pieces are original compositions by the authors unless stated otherwise.

Contents

1. Carnival jig

KB & DB

2. Spic and span

KB & DB

Variation: try playing with 2 semiquavers to each note:

3. Out of the question

Play questions and answers in this duet, returning to the chorus after each verse.
Make up and write down a question and answer of your own in the 3rd verse. Add your own dynamics!

Confident

KB & DB

4. Stop—start

KB & DB

5. River song

KB & DB

6. Overture

A Baroque celebration

KB & DB

Allegro

7. Going fourth

Andante

KB & DB

8. City streets

KB & DB

Driving

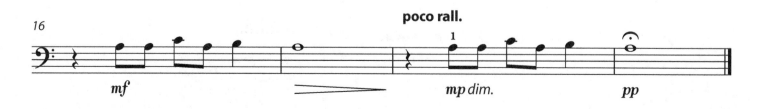

9. Minuet

Allegretto

W. A. Mozart (1756–91)

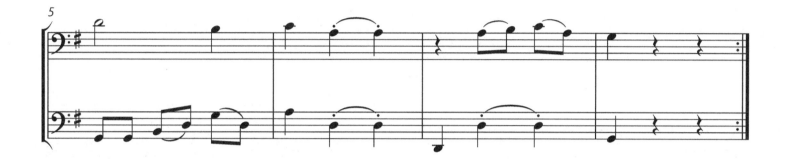

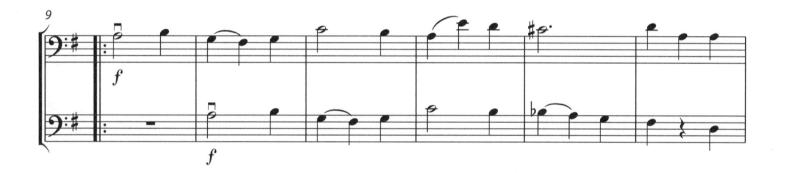

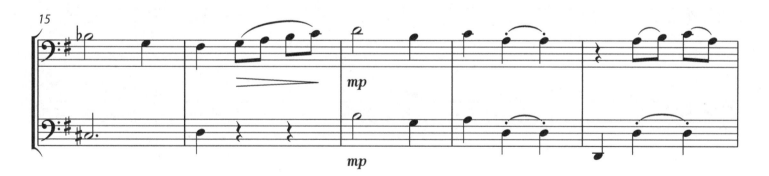

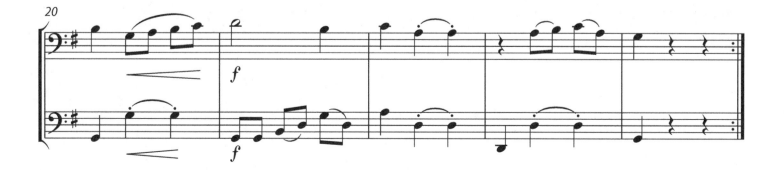

10. Metro line

KB & DB

11. Falling leaves

KB & DB

Warm up

Play a G major scale in the rumba rhythm:

Swing low, sweet cha - ri - ot,__ com-in' for to car-ry me home.

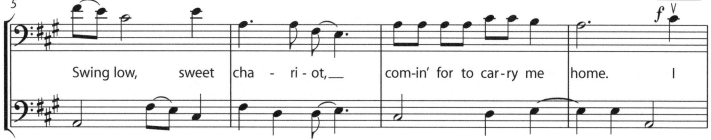

Swing low, sweet cha - ri - ot,__ com-in' for to car-ry me home. I

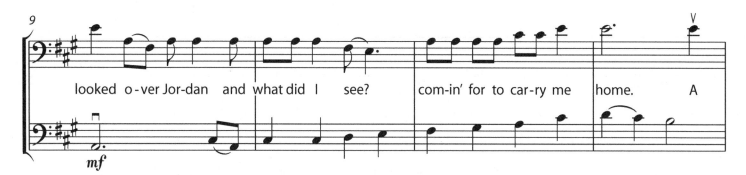

looked o - ver Jor-dan and what did I see? com-in' for to car-ry me home. A

band of an - gels com-in' af-ter me,__ com-in' for to car-ry me home.

Play the second chorus as a canon, with the second part entering after a minim at *.
Count carefully in bar 20! Also try as a canon in 3 or 4 parts.

14. Night shift

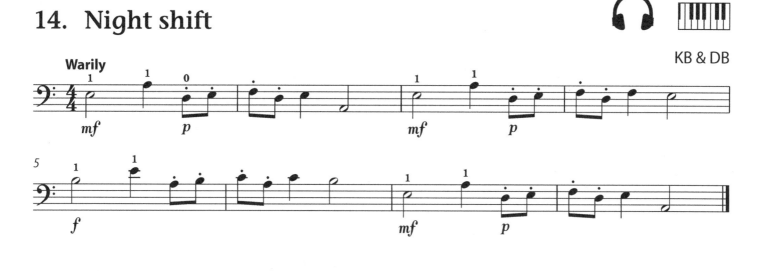

KB & DB

15. Le Tambourin

J. Ph. Rameau (1683–1764)
(adapted)

A tambourin was a lively 18th-century French dance, often accompanied by pipe and tabor.

16. Scarborough Fair

English trad.

Wistful

17. Beyond the horizon

Very calm and still

KB & DB

mp legatissimo

18. Sto me

Bulgarian trad.

With energy

A backing track for a version of the piece transposed up a fifth to A minor is available on the Companion Website. Try playing it by ear—here's the start:

19. Bourrée

G. H. Stölzel (1690–1749)

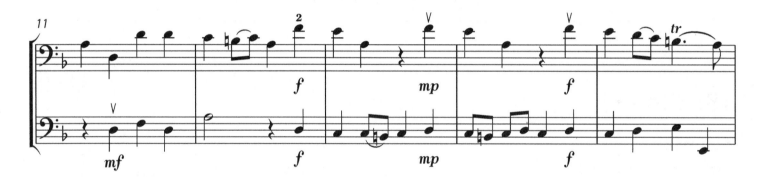

Adapted from the Clavierbüchlein for Wilhelm Friedemann Bach.

20. Andante

Edward Elgar (1857–1934)

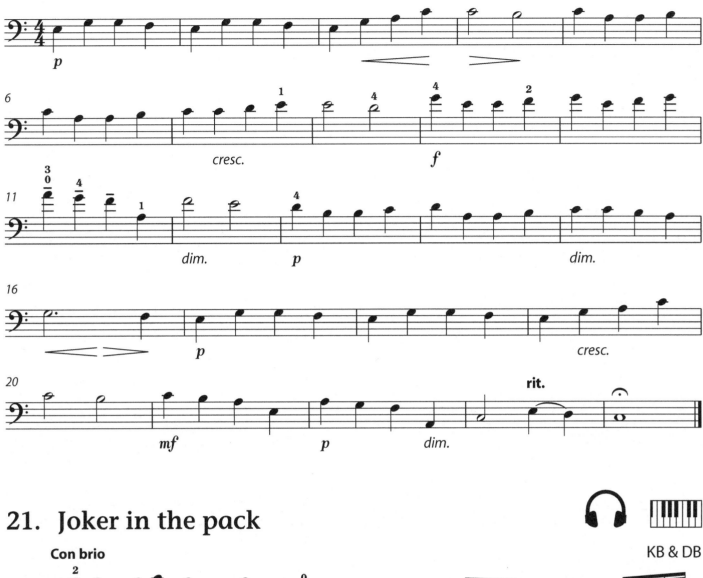

21. Joker in the pack

KB & DB

Con brio

22. Sarabande

G. F. Handel (1685–1759)
(adapted)

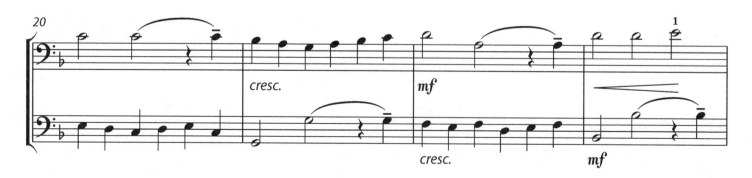

18

23. Comin' home

KB & DB

24. Sprint finish

KB & DB

25. In memory

(for Eileen)

KB & DB

26. Some day

27. Wild West

KB & DB

Warm up

Sort out the F naturals and F sharps, and B naturals and B flats in this piece before you start.

28. Je pense à toi

(for Clare)

KB & DB

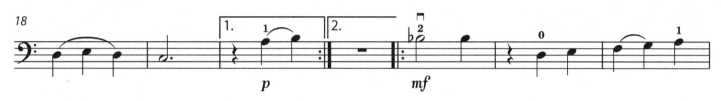

Think of the timbre and dynamic changes as you play the repeat phrase in 1st and 4th position.

29. Russian wedding

KB & DB

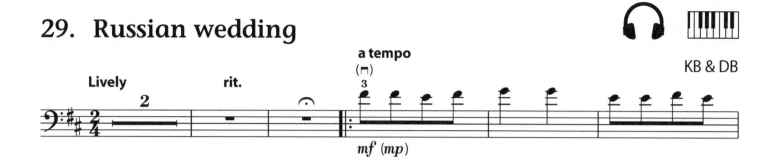

30. Two Songs from Dichterliebe

1. The lovely month of May

Robert Schumann (1810–56)
(adapted)

2. The rose and the lily

31. Latin nights

Tango

KB & DB

32. 4th dimension

KB & DB

Warm up

Play an F major scale in the rhythm of the opening bar—don't play on the first beat, and watch the accents!

33. Fifth Avenue

(for Iain)

KB & DB

34. Seventh heaven

Dominant seventh study

KB & DB

$\downarrow$
$\times$ Tap your cello with your left hand.

35. Jubilate Deo

Play this round in 2 or more parts, entering at *:

W. A. Mozart (1756–91)

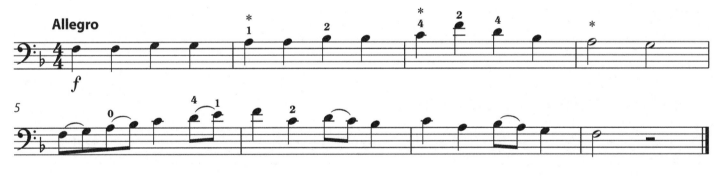

36. Banuwa

Play this round in 2 or more parts, entering at *:

African

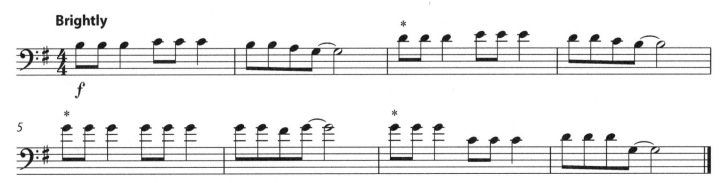

Scales and Arpeggios

A major scale 1 octave

A major arpeggio 1 octave

B♭ major scale 1 octave

B♭ major arpeggio 1 octave

C harmonic minor scale 1 octave

C melodic minor scale 1 octave

C minor arpeggio 1 octave

G harmonic minor scale 1 octave

G melodic minor scale 1 octave

G minor arpeggio 1 octave

D major scale 2 octaves

D major arpeggio 2 octaves

C major scale 2 octaves

C major arpeggio 2 octaves

D harmonic minor scale 2 octaves

D melodic minor scale 2 octaves

D minor arpeggio 2 octaves

G major scale 2 octaves

G major arpeggio 2 octaves

F major scale 2 octaves

F major arpeggio 2 octaves

Dominant 7th in the key of F

Dominant 7th in the key of C

Dominant 7th in the key of G